Kolorblind Soul

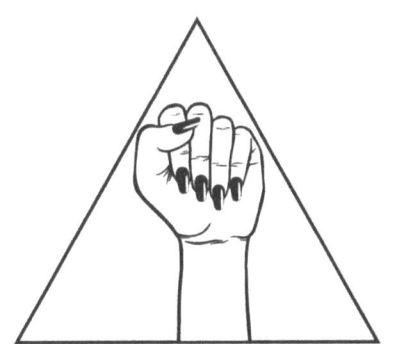

Poet U.B.

Kolorblind Soul
Copyright © 2020 by Selena "Poet U.B." Garcia
All rights reserved.

This book or any portion thereof may not be reproduced or used in any manner whatsoever without the express written permission of the publisher except for the use of brief quotations in a book review.

Printed in the United States of America
First Printing, 2020

ISBN:
978-0-9975711-3-4 (paperback)
978-0-9975711-4-1 (eBook)
978-0-9975711-5-8 (audiobook)

Published by Selena "Poet U.B." Garcia
Urban Butterflii / Poet U.B.
Pomona / Inglewood, CA

Cover Design Team: Selena Garcia, Matthew Garcia
Editing by Selena Garcia
Interior Design by Penoaks Publishing,
http://penoaks.com
Photos by Dominic Young Photography, Yasmine J Photography, Poet U.B. Publishing
Cover photo: AJ Lamor Productions
Logo Graphic Designer: Jovee Edwards
Used by permission. All rights reserved.
www.PoetUB.com

My goal
is to inspire you to love,
be empathetic and embrace differences in
a genuine attempt to eliminate racism and prejudice.

Poet U.B.

Dedicated to

all with melanin in our skin
who are targets of racial injustice,
prejudice and racism because of appearance.

Judgement often causes misunderstanding and hatred.
Observing one's character and not judging by appearance
allows for brotherhood to exist organically
becoming our reality rather than just a dream.
I believe that racism is humanity's greatest downfall, but
I also believe that showing love and empathy
is the beginning of restoring humanity.

And to my precious angel, Jelani Woods-Garcia.

You made me believe in love when I thought I lost hope. You made me remember God when I lost my faith. You made me understand how strong I am when I thought I was going to fall apart. You made me overstand the meaning of unconditional love. Your heartbeat was the most beautiful music my ears ever heard. I never had the opportunity to hear you laugh, cry or say your first words, take your first steps, see your first smile, but you gave me something NO ONE can ever take away from me. YOU made me a mother. And from the suffering I endured after losing you, I have emerged as one of the strongest and resilient souls I know. Now, because of you, my mission is to provide others with a different point of view, in hopes that they chose to love and embrace others without judgement.

Table of Contents

Preface | 9
Introduction | 11
<u>change</u>
Change Gone Come | 15

Part One: Discrimination and Prejudice | 17
Sometimes. . . | 19
Helpless | 22
Torn Apart | 23
Will It Ever Be | 24
<u>anger</u>
<u>rebel</u>
<u>impetuous</u>
After. . . | 26
Fakes | 27
Dear Mom | 28
<u>bond</u>
When. . . | 33
Unforgettable | 35
Baby Brother | 37
Back My Way | 39
I'm Sorry | 40
Been Replaced | 41
A Better Man | 43
<u>self-doubt</u>
After. . . | 46
Dear Lord (What Is It All For?) | 48
<u>unconditional</u>
I do not. . . | 54
Her Man | 55
<u>injustice</u>
<u>prejudice</u>
<u>ignorance</u>
Witnessing prejudice. . . | 57

Twelve | *60*
Wrongfully Accused | *62*
Spit | *63*
Moonlight Blues | *65*
With No Disrespect | *67*
This War | *69*
Our Youth | *70*
Didn't Know | *73*
Trying To Understand | *74*
Silent But Deadly | *76*
Cold World | *78*
<u>ethnicity</u>
<u>difference</u>
Many times. . . | *81*
Barbers | *82*
Correct This | *84*
<u>guilty</u>
<u>association</u>
It's extremely difficult to express. . . | *86*
Guilty By Association | *88*
That One Day | *89*

Part Two: Love and Empathy | 93
I Can Only Be Me | *95*
<u>spiritual</u>
<u>divine</u>
<u>connection</u>
<u>oss</u>
When you connect with someone. . . | *97*
Me And Mal | *98*
U.B. OSS | *99*
<u>side</u>
<u>represent</u>
In your community, | *101*
Paving The Way | *102*
Sides | *105*
Targets | *106*
Chains | *107*
Given, Token | *109*

Ambiguous | 111

<u>strength</u>
<u>overcome</u>

In dealing with racism, prejudice and ignorance, | 113
Stronger Than You | 115
Stand Proud | 117
I Love Me | 119
Enlightenment | 121

<u>love</u>
<u>embrace</u>

Love is one of the most. . . | 123
Colorblind Love | 125
Treasure | 126
Love Hazard | 129
Can't Get Enough | 133
How I Love You | 135
She | 136
Forever Reflected | 137
My Little Girl | 138
Early Bird | 139

<u>empathy</u>
<u>legacy</u>
<u>impact</u>

Empathy is. . . | 141
Let Me | 143
We Matter | 145
Soul Strings | 147
Fingerprints | 149
Acknowledgements | 152
About The Author | 159

Preface

KOLORBLIND SOUL

Why did I spell colorblind with a K?

Two of my children's names begin with a K and a S. So I chose to change the spelling of colorblind to begin with a K. My children have everything to do with my goals and my "Why" in my life. They are the reasons I hustle so hard, the reasons I try my best and give extra effort even when I feel as though I have nothing left to give. They are my inspiration to promote my passion for love and unity. They are the reasons I am so strong. I believe that my children are living proof that unity in love can produce amazing, phenomenal, talented people and extraordinarily special bonds. I have always believed in equality, fairness and not judging people by their appearance. These are things I try to instill in my children as well. I want my children to understand that, yes, there is racism, discrimination, prejudice and hate that exist in this world, but we have the power to change it. We can obtain the knowledge and create a powerful, positive impact on our future. We can do this as long as we believe in something greater, a greater future for ourselves and our future generations. Our time for a new revolution is now. We must teach our children that they have the power to learn, grow and become strong leaders that can create change and better themselves and their communities.

Kolorblind Soul was created from situations that have inspired me to tell my story, my point of view, my beliefs. It was created from emotions and feelings of pain, sorrow, confusion, joy, happiness, understanding, love and empathy.

So with that being said, everything I am, everything I do is for our future. . . for OUR Revolution.

Kolorblind Soul Revolution.

Introduction

"Stick to your own kind. . ."

I've heard this more times than I can count, not just verbally but through actions as well. People tell me I should be ashamed of outside breeding. Breeding? I'm not an animal. People told me having mixed children was wrong. Somehow along my journey, it was instilled in me to not give a fuck about what others thought about me or my decisions. Now, I realize that the way I addressed situations and how I viewed things wasn't always the wisest outlook on life, but I refused to let others' opinions of me shape my life or change my values. I have always been strong minded and willing to stand up for what I believed to be right. I refuse to be part of the racism problem. I try to instill in our youth these days that prejudices and racism are wrong. So even though I stand strong in my beliefs, I also acknowledge when there is a need for change.

The only constant in this life besides God, in my opinion. . . Change.

Hate changes things for the worst. I think we need to change for the better as humans. We need to unify in order just to survive these days. We need to understand that as a whole, meaning all people of color, that together we are much stronger people. We need to take a look in the mirror and understand that this change we've been soul-searching for needs to first come from within. I am a firm believer that LOVE can move mountains and produce miracles. When you love with your whole heart and soul, selflessly, you are willing to do anything. We need to love ourselves enough to change this race war. We will never win, if we proceed to act with hate and selfishness. This will only continue to divide ourselves into smaller groups creating an image of a weaker frontline in this race war. People will see us as easier to defeat and try to conquer us more often.

Discriminatory events and situations that are happening these days, truly disturb my soul to it's core due to all the killings, racist based bullying, stereotyping, police brutality. . . I understand that these issues are not brand new, however these issues are at a point where we need to rise up and stand for respect, acceptance of differences, unity and understanding. We need to fight against racism, discrimination and prejudice to give our youth a chance to live in a world where equality truly exists and isn't just a great idea written down like a promissory note.

I can't think of anything better than to share my God-given talent. I feel this in the depths of my soul that we should change the way things are now. I am only one person, so I need you. My message to you, to our elders, to our youth, to our future. . .

Change. Change hate into love. Love conquers all. Accept others. Embrace different cultures. Appreciate others' lifestyles. Unity is scarce. Let's make it abundant. This is time for OUR revolution.

OUR Kolorblind Soul Revolution.

Kolorblind Soul.

change

verb
1. make or become different.

noun
2. the act or an instance of making or becoming different.

Change Gone Come

She looks at her reflection
But her sense of direction
Is misguided by her lack of
Confidence. Mistreated by love
Needs nurturing, her soul neglected
But before she can be rejected
She hides, self-pity swallows her whole
Allowing more obstacles to block her goals.
She takes one more look
And that's all it took
To catch a glimpse of that passion that burns
Of the artistic soul that yearns
For fulfillment not in a physical form
She now stands in the eye of the storm
Ready for change to be lifted from here
It's all up to you. Change is here, my dear.

Part One

Discrimination and Prejudice

Sometimes...

you have to go through obstacles or through a personal struggle in order to get to where you want to be or to gain knowledge of something in your current life. You might have not previously noticed that a change or growth was needed had you not been placed in that predicament. An inner struggle within yourself has caused you to have a hard time making a decision. However, it can also be an outer struggle where someone else is trying to force you to make a decision by giving you an ultimatum. Sometimes people will try to make the decision for you even when you both know that the transgression imposed upon you is wrong. My motto is and has always been, 'You should definitely follow your heart'. Although a lot of times when you choose to follow **only** your heart, you face more obstacles that place you in a position where you have to make difficult decisions. Not always do people try to be empathetic, see your point of view, your situation, nor are they open-minded enough at least to try to understand.

There are many multi-ethnic families nowadays, but interracial relationships haven't always been openly accepted. Not to say people all are for it now, because it still causes families to be torn apart, causes conflict between races who do not agree and causes heartache for those who love extremely hard. But some people do not obtain the capacity to understand what it means to love someone no matter what color their skin is. Love is love, no matter what. And unfortunately, sometimes you have to choose between two different loves, family love and romantic love. Relationships and friendships that are built throughout the childhood years are then put through the test of loyalty. Unfortunately, because it's hard to choose between family and romantic love, bonds are broken. No matter how strong you feel the foundation is, not all things are guaranteed. Oftentimes when a decision is made for you, all you can do is embrace the situation as best as you can and try to move forward accordingly. Now, this is not as easy as it may seem, but in no way am I suggesting that you should conform to their beliefs or views. Be strong, stand up for yourself, and stand for a cause. Believe in your decision as you follow your heart. And even though you stand strong, sometimes, there's an automatic void that appears. It hurts like hell and doesn't seem like anyone can ever fill it. But the power is in your hands. You and only you have the power to persevere.

There will be stress and heartache when re-establishing a life for yourself especially when it has been caused by ignorance, misunderstandings, misplaced hate, racism and prejudice. I fear that too many young people are put in these types of positions to where they are excommunicated by their family all because of the race, skin color, culture or ethnicity of the person who they love. I know because I was in that position in an early period of my life. It was a very lonely and confusing time. Emotional situations at times, can feel painful and unbearable. Yet they happen every day. There needs to be a change in the thought process to unlearn prejudices and racism in order to open minds. This lack of humanity in our own communities is sending a message to others outside of our communities, who already judge and look down on us, that we are separating within. If it seems as though we create separation within, we give them an image that we can be easily broken. Even though it may feel that way at times, we need to learn how we can grow stronger and come together, love and embrace one another and above all walk in unity.

Wrongdoings will continue to happen every day, but we cannot shut down and give in. Although we must be strong, we still have to allow ourselves to feel. We may feel anger, pain, betrayal, deceit, hurt,
confusion... But you still have to allow yourself to feel. Sometimes you may feel helpless or alone, and even though you don't want things to go a certain way or may wish you could make others have an open mind, there are just some things we can't control.
But if the transgressions of others can be addressed with positive outlooks, open minds and education, some relationships can be repaired.

Some transgressions imposed upon you can feel unforgivable.
Some transgressions can be forgiven.

Always remember how you have been trespassed and how it made you feel. Be open-minded enough to not impose similar transgressions on others.

Helpless

Isolated
Sometimes my feelings seem to have faded
Deny me
You might as well crucify me
Contemplation
Leads to not even one solution
I'm helpless, I'm helpless!
Five
The years, alone, I've had to survive
Words
Never spoken, never heard
every day
Wonder, if you pick up the phone, what you'd say
But. . .
I'm helpless
I'm H E L P L E S S!

Torn Apart

They don't understand.
So I'm torn.
My ground, I'll stand.
It's my turn
To experience loving
Someone who loves me,
But the hurt is cutting
Beyond the deepest deep.
Exchanging love for in love
Will it last, I'm unsure
But I've had enough
Of them trying to interfere
He is my heartbeat
So they have to understand
They'd rather retreat
Than be part of the plan
Why does color play a part?
Why does it make a difference?
Why must you tear our family apart
Because of your ignorance?

Will It Ever Be

If I could only find the words to explain
Why every day I live, it rains.
This pain, this pain, this pain!
It's as if my heart's been brutally slain.
This headache never-ending,
I can't remember the beginning.
When? When will it go away?
There's nothing that anyone can say.
Today is just another horrible day.
It hurts so bad just to pray.
I'm helpless, my hands are tied.
So many days and nights I've cried,
But nothing seems to help my heart.
I've looked everywhere for a new start.
My world is slowly falling apart.
I feel that I will never be part
Of what my heart once dreamed of. . .
A life and family full of love.

anger

noun
1. a strong feeling of annoyance, irritation, or hostility.

rebel

noun
1. a person who rises in opposition or armed resistance against an established government or authority.

verb

2. to rise in opposition or resistance against an established government or authority.

impetuous

adjective
1. acting or done quickly and without thought or care.

After...

feeling helpless and hopeless as a result of transgressions being imposed upon you, you can sometimes feel angry, rebellious or even impetuous. Many people deal with these feelings differently but you should never allow anyone to disregard your feelings. You are allowed to feel any kind of way. Just be mindful of how you react after acknowledging these feelings. Not all situations or instances require an immediate response, especially when you're upset. Most often a response when you're upset will create a more hostile outcome. When I was younger I dealt with these negative feelings and other negative situations with sarcasm, plenty, plenty of slick talking sarcasm. Many times saying hurtful things, but all honest feelings in the heat of the moment. Some of the comments made, probably would have been better left unsaid, but sometimes you really need to express your anger in order to let it out. Harboring these negative feelings is never good for your mental, emotional or spiritual health. However, I learned that with writing as my outlet, I could use my sarcasm to express myself without directly hurting anyone's feelings. Keep in mind as I stated before, some transgressions imposed upon you can "feel" unforgivable. I know it is hard to forgive when someone has hurt you, but it doesn't have to remain negative. You can turn it into a positive. Get it out creatively or productively. Some transgressions can be forgiven even when the other person does not, will not or cannot apologize.

Fakes

I wake up, cold sweat
Him screaming at me: "nigger lover" repeats
At first I regretted the day we ever met
Because I ended up on the streets
But I don't. I don't regret the love we shared
There was a reason we were paired
But why couldn't they understand
The experience was spiritual
It wasn't ever planned
But in love I was a fool
I didn't want to leave
Leaving home, I was forced to
Now every day I grieve
But again I'd do it if I had to
I just wish they could have realized
I know they would've learned
but instead they justified
their hate and it was confirmed
Although their actions are inexcusable
And they remained stubborn and juvenile
They refused to see diversity is so beautiful
My heart may hurt a while
But I can't take back my past
Even though my soul aches
And the love I had didn't last
At least now I know who are the fakes.

I share this point of view only because since written, forgiveness has allowed relationships to be mended, empathy has allowed open communication and love has allowed God to restore so much of what had been lost. Not all decisions made under an impetuous mindset are permanent. Transgressions can be forgiven.

Dear Mom

August 17, 1999

Dear Mom,
Why is my preference a sin?
With you, I will never win,
But I am satisfied.
Yes, I may have lied,
But you don't understand.
Now I have the upper hand
Wait. . . Why must I apologize?
It's not as if you don't tell lies
What about the weed you smoke?
You go in your room, take a few tokes
Then come out calm and cool
You just don't know your lies have you looking like a fool
Even my little brother knows what you do
When you say you're cleaning for an hour or two
What about when you were a kid?
Remember all the shit you did?
If you did, you would see
I ain't like you, trust me!
Denying it is just another fuckin' lie I have to hear
My eyes are too damn tired to cry another tear
I blocked out so much of my childhood
That's why alone I always stood

Now I look at this situation I'm in
And honestly I don't see sin in color of skin
Conditional: why is your love this way
I don't say a word; one day you'll pay
Karma is a bitch like me
Or at least that's what you see
Why do you insist on trying to control?
You're only digging yourself into a hole
People will soon realize your hate
Everything after that is fate
One thing I can't seem to understand. . .
You wanted me to be alone on the street
Why? Maybe so I could get my ass beat. . .
Not everyone is as ignorant as you
A lot of people love me more than you do
And too many people care about me
I'm sure by now you see
That I don't need you anymore
I've found everything I was looking for
A mother-figure who knows me
And takes time out to listen
A father-figure who is always there
And with me his knowledge he shares
It's funny how much I've grown
I would have left sooner if I would've known
It would be this great
I wanted to live in another state
When I lived at home
My only escape was writing poems
Now I know how to express myself

When this talent brings me wealth
I will thank you for being a bitch
Because without you I wouldn't be rich
You might apologize
Because you'll have realized
That you were not right
Then I'll have you removed from my sight
I love you and I always will
But I'll always remember how you made me feel
At this stage in my life
When the only thing that's between us is this strife
Color of skin = sin: I still can't understand why
But now I'm fuckin' tired of trying
I'm not sorry that my choices make you cry
Although they probably don't even phase you when you're high
Remember when you got married to dad
And inside all the happiness you had
One day that's what I will feel
And I will know that my love is real
I don't know when that will be
Or if you'll be around to see
When I have kids. I know you'll regret
That my husband and I ever met
But just to let you know one last thing
When someone proposes to me, the ring
Will be from a "colored" man
Maybe you won't understand
Until I'm finally dead
That's when you'll regret all the fuckin' lies you've said
But until then we'll never know
So for now, on with the show.

bond

noun
1. a thing used to tie something or to fasten things together.
2. a force or feeling that unites people; a common emotion or interest.

When...

you have a close bond with a sibling, family member or a close friend and it's forced to end neither by you or by the other person, each person learns a coping mechanism. They do this in order to deal with any unfamiliar feelings that may surface. Being in a new situation, not everyone knows how to react or move forward. Sometimes you choose a sport or hobby to occupy the time or to distract your mind. Sometimes you choose to befriend someone similar to the person you lost in order to fill a void. Although the voids aren't always fulfilled, sometimes these coping mechanisms help. And finally, when you are able to reunite with those you've been separated from, sometimes insecurities get the better of your feelings and make things appear as something they are not. I can recall feeling extremely hurt after so much time had passed and I missed so much from my family's lives. I can recall feeling devastated and thinking that I had been temporarily replaced, but life and time waits for no one. One thing that should never be doubted is that the love that once existed in a friendship is never lost especially when a forced decision is made without consent from either side. Once your relationship has been reconciled you will realize that even though both sides had to move on and grow, love still exists. It may not be or feel exactly the same, but when the love is strong, a loving friendship will always remain. Don't doubt it. Unconditional love is an irreplaceable bond that no one can take from you no matter how hard they try. During the period you spend away from your family or loved ones, it may cause pain to your heart and soul. Some days are easier than others. Some days are so difficult that it's painful and difficult to simply breathe. But remember that you should never allow these experiences to change your heart negatively. You have to push through and try to grow and learn from these experiences.

Unforgettable

We had tears in our eyes
As we said our half goodbyes
I just wished you'd say
Don't leave, please stay;
But those words never came
I know our pain was the same
The animosity towards the oppressor I aim
But you are not the one to blame
Instead you said I'd help you
But Mom will be mad at me too;
I understood your reasoning
I couldn't believe I was leaving
Even though you may have thought I was wrong
You supported and loved me all along
That was never doubted
Even when my judgment was clouded
I loved him, why couldn't they see?
But these two places I couldn't be
They said I wasn't allowed to stay
Unless from me he stayed away
Him, I couldn't call, see or be around
So because of love, a new place was found
I cried the whole way there
Tears flooded my eyes as into space I stared
I couldn't believe I was free
But now a huge pain was inflicted upon me
These two different loves tearing me apart
I couldn't stand it, so I had to make a new start
But I lost so much when I had to leave
I won't lose my best friend; my heart believed
That woman's words ran through my mind
"Finally you're leaving"; I left everything behind

I truly thought it was right for me
Even though no one else could see
I know now it was worth it since the first day
To God every day I'd pray
I prayed for God to make you strong
And to let me know if I was wrong
Eventually God gave me strength and hope
Every day I had to find a new way to cope
I've gone through quite a lot since then
And I made sure that every day ended with Amen.
Most nights I cry myself to sleep
Because the emptiness runs so deep
I need my sister, best friend in my life once more
Our friendship we need to restore
I can't ever give you back all the time
We lost, but my friendship and love I'll combine
And hopefully you'll find it in your heart
To accept my apology and make a new start

I worried endlessly
But I never doubted your loyalty
I always knew that through the misery
You'd be one to show sincerity
I'm sorry that I made things difficult
Everything was my fault
Even though we're two different people
My heart knows that each other we'll never outgrow
So I say to you now
You want to know How?
It's not like I left on my own
It was a forced choice, to you, left unknown
But I'll take all the blame
Because out of all of this, I'm proud of who I became
A strong woman, mother, and friend
I just hope one day my actions you'll comprehend.

Baby Brother

I am sorry I left you,
If you could only understand. . .

I stare at pictures of you,
If I could just hold your hand. . .

I want you to know
My world is still filled with you
I want to watch you grow
My baby boy is you
When you become a teen
I will try to explain
When, where, and what exactly you've seen
I live without you and it drives me insane
I am so helpless now
When it comes to you
I really wish I could prove how
When it rains it POURS, in my life without you
I pray every day
I know God is protecting you
Have fun being a kid, go play
I will be here waiting for you
It felt shattered, my heart
When I left that night
It was clear that we would be apart
When my life is dark, you are my light.

I do not want you to forget

When I sang you the jacket song;
I do not want you to forget
My love for you is so very strong
I remember we were at the store
And we saw your old grandma there
I remember you always asking for more
And then, with me you would share

I held you when you slept
I made sure you were comfy
I tried to comfort you when you wept
I was always happy when you were with me.
I cannot wait for the day
That I get to see you
I can't tell you how much I pray
For that dream to come true.

Back My Way

Friendship is hard to come by
But I found it in you, My Sister
All these nights without you I cry
My heart aches from missing My Sister
Our bond was growing strong
But for now we are apart
I know that it won't be long
And keeping in touch is a start
High? Low?
We'd race to ask every night
Every day we grow closer
Even though you're out of my sight
Sometimes I sit and wonder why
I am not able to see you

I know the reason, and now I cry
Love. One day it will be you
There's a feeling, very strong
Deep down within my heart
I know that it is very wrong
For anyone to try to keep us apart
You're my only sister
And I will always be here for you
You're my baby sister
No matter what it is you do
You are my Best Friend
And every day to God I pray
That one day he will send
My one and only baby sister back my way.

I'm Sorry

I miss you with all my heart.
It kills me every day we're apart.

I love you so.
This I know you know,
But it's hard every day.
There's always so much to you I'd like to say,
But I hope you can understand
The decision was not in my hands.
It was something that was destiny.
It was how God made me feel free
From all of my unhappiness and uncertainty.
I had to go through a lot to finally see
That this is my place in life,
And yes, I'm a mother not a wife
Yes, mistakes, I've made some,
But a stronger woman I've become.

So I hope you can open your heart to see
That all I want is for you to forgive me
For all the pain and strife I've caused you.
This apology and my love for you have always been true.

Been Replaced

Isn't is crazy when
You feel just lazy, And
Nothing can heal the scar, And
You've traveled so far, And
You feel you've been replaced
By an even prettier face, And
You want to curse them,
But,
You can't be mad at them
So,
What do you do?
What do you do?
Well I just think about
How I took a different route
And
Now I face the music
But It just hurts within

Listen
It's supposed to be me. . .
It's supposed to be me. . .
Yet
Not by choice I was gone
Way way way too long
But
It shouldn't hurt so bad
I shouldn't be so sad
I should understand
But. . . I don't.
Cause someone's taken my place
I feel I've been replaced
Now I doubt myself
But I can only be me
And
I guess it's not good enough for you
But I don't hold it against you
So, will you accept me now?
Or Is she really your sista'?

A Better Man

No one will ever understand
Although, I'm glad you're a better man
It still brings me pain; you see?
Or maybe it's just jealousy
She was there when I couldn't be
I just wish you could see. . .
I asked HIM that He'd look after you
I asked HIM that He'd protect you
I knew he wouldn't let me down
And that's probably when she came around
Don't get the wrong impression
I'm not going through a depression
There's just an aching pain
That especially hurts when it's cold and it rains
Nothing can heal it
You just have to deal with it
No one will ever understand
Although, I'm glad you're a better man
I'm proud of who you've become
And to this relationship I must succumb
I have to face the fact

She was concrete; I was abstract
There's a wall it's hard for me to see beyond
We always had a special bond
I pray that it still exists
But I shouldn't reminisce
Just be in the present
My feelings I must not misrepresent
It's hard that she was accepted when I was not
To be there, so many times I've fought
I'm still fighting the war every day
And every day I continue to pray
No one will ever understand
Although, I'm glad you're a better man.

self-doubt

noun
1. lack of confidence in oneself and one's abilities.

After...

you go through traumas in your life, it becomes harder to put your best foot forward all the time. You tend to doubt yourself and oftentimes lose your way. You can lose focus and just go into survival mode, autopilot if you will. You doubt yourself, you doubt your decisions. In a sense, you become lost, a wanderer. Being alone, on your own without family or friends to turn to, you can become vulnerable to many situations. When you are young, alone and have yet to experience the world fully, there is a greater chance that you will be vulnerable and naive. We need to seek knowledge, self-worth and educate ourselves and each other. Being black and brown the world already sees us as if we are less than. So the world supplies us with an easy path to self-doubt, negativity and self destruction. We need to not take that road. Ever.

Racism and prejudices have a domino effect of negative influences. Ignorance is the leader, the first domino to fall. It tends to overpower other dominoes and activate self-doubt, low self-esteem, lack of self-worth, depression, loneliness. . . which leaves you in a position of feeling broken without guidance. All of the protective walls you believed to have been impenetrable have now vanished completely. You are not guarded. You may not feel safe. There are now so many questions because so many things seem unclear. All anyone in that situation is looking for is for some type of confirmation that love still exists in the world and that there is hope for unity and family once again. It is ok to have questions. It is ok to be lost sometimes. But you make sure you ask all the questions you need to in order to get back on track. Self-doubt can begin a path to growth. It can lead you on a road to self-discovery and understanding. When you doubt yourself and begin searching, your search can lead you to learn more about who you are, where you want to be and who you want to become. You have to be open to explore and put yourself in a vulnerable position to be better. It's a difficult road sometimes as we face harsh realities and things we may feel uncomfortable with. But this is part of life. It's growth. If you want to be better, you have to be open to change. Not all change is bad. . . Change can be great, if you allow it.

Dear Lord
(What Is It All For?)

Dear Lord,
I finally figured out life is a double edged sword
I need you to show me the door
Show me. What is it all for?

You showed me how to be an angel to many
Although for some reason I can't see
A future like this one
At times I'm unsure if I'm done
You, the giver of life, gave me part of you
He's not here now and I don't know what to do
I feel like I have nothing of my own
And every day I feel more and more alone
Overwhelming emotions boil inside
Yet I take each day with stride
Or at least that's how I make it appear
But deep inside I harbor many fears

Dear Lord,
I finally figured out life is a double edged sword
I need you to show me the door
Show me. What is it all for?

Will anyone ever love me?
Will anyone truly care?
Can anyone find a cure

Or a remedy for being this scared?
Why can't he be mine?
Why do I always cry?
Will I ever find the one
Before my life is done?
What if I die before I wake?
How many times will I make the same mistake?
What about my family
Will they accept me for me?
I don't want to die alone
I don't care if I'm well known
I just want to take care of my kids
And let them do all the things I never did Will my kids love me?
Will I ever feel free?
What if I can't figure it out?
Should I try to take a new route?
Why do I get so easily depressed?
What if I fail a very important test?
Why do I smile to cover my tears?
I've been doing that for over 9 years.
Will anyone ever understand my pain?
Who will be my sunshine when it rains?
Will I ever truly get over it?
Please allow me to be that fortunate.

Dear Lord,
I finally figured out life is a double-edged sword
I need you to show me the door
Show me. What is it all for?

Am I going out on a limb
To tell him I love him?
Will he love me forever
Or will he leave me for Her?
Will I eventually fall apart?
If I do, will I be able to make a new start?
Are my people around me true?
If they're not, what the hell will I do?
What if I don't find my way
And end up somewhere I don't want to stay?
Why am I always so nice?
Why can't I sometimes be cold as ice?
You have shown me to survive, to cope.
That's probably why I possess a small amount of hope,
But right now I feel like I've been drug through the mud
And my entire body is covered in my blood
This life I lead breaks me down more and more each day
So now I look up in the sky and to YOU I pray...

Dear Lord,
Show me, what is it all for?

unconditional

adjective
1. not subject to any conditions.

I do not. . .

like politics and rarely do I engage in them. I do pay attention to the news and policies that will affect myself and my family. Most times that I have heard a political conversation, people are excluded from a conversation or attacked because of an opinion that the majority in that particular group doesn't agree with. The conversation may heat up, but then it is forgotten about and we move on. More often these days, people have become extra sensitive to every issue and we disconnect from others just because we do not share the same political views or share the same opinion on a matter. Rather than being open minded and trying to empathize or at least gain an understanding, many people just choose to stop communication or shut others out. But being in an interracial relationship where one person firmly believes in a political party that hates the race, culture or ethnic background of the person they are dating, becomes more than an obstacle. It is now the deciding factor of a future for a couple. Years ago, the same relationship was labeled as "fated through unconditional love to last forever", has now become conditional. How can the one person you love the most, believe in the words, views and strategies of a political leader who despises and opposes everything you stand for, everything you have come from, everything you are? How do you get past that and move on? How do you remain in a relationship with the weight of the world placed on whether you remain together or break up? How do you overcome this? Or do you?

Her Man

I can't stand her
but I love that she loves me
I don't like her
because with her I don't feel free
she doesn't understand
I don't even know if she tries
she used to be my number one fan
now I feel like she always lies
the differences are beginning
to surface with no remorse
what I believed to be the beginning
seems to have run its course
she loves him, all orange
and I love every other shade
nothing rhymes with orange
so maybe I've been played
I'm taken for granted
to satisfy her need for company
I've become disenchanted
on political views we don't agree
so I'll take my bags and walk
because I can't seem to understand
her views or the dialect in which she talks
running different races, I'm no longer her man.

injustice

noun
1. unfair treatment: a situation in which the rights of a person or a group of people are ignored; to treat in an unfair way

prejudice

noun
1. preconceived opinion that is not based on reason or actual experience.
2. unreasonable feelings, opinions, or attitudes, especially of a hostile nature, regarding an ethnic, racial, social, or religious group.

ignorance

noun
1. lack of knowledge or information.

Witnessing prejudice...

and ignorance on television and social media is hurtful and harmful. When you experience social injustice, prejudice and ignorance first hand, it opens your mind up to a world that you may have thought may never affect you. Once that door opens, it will never shut. There are just some things you cannot unsee. Some experiences cannot be erased no matter how hard we try to forget or dismiss them. There are so many examples of racial injustice, ignorance and prejudice but what really affects society today is the lack of morality. People are not born racist, prejudice or ignorant. These are learned behaviors. They are taught through direct lessons or learned through experiences of being around others who displayed racism towards others. As people who are constantly targeted, we need to educate our youth in order for them not to be taken advantage of. Show them empathy, teach them to be open-minded, to have no judgement, to embrace everyone's differences, be proud of where they come from and be mindful of their actions and words so they can use them to make a positive change. If we can do that and embrace one another openly, we can become a stronger force than the opposition who view us as targets. One thing I can't seem to come to terms with or accept, is why a lot of hate, dislike and prejudices come from your own race or ethnic background. People who share in your struggles should also be the first to understand or have empathy for your situation or your preferences. It's perfectly acceptable that they do not choose the same for themselves, but the least they can do is have empathy and try to understand. You shouldn't feel like you have to always defend yourself or explain yourself especially around people such as your family who should love you unconditionally.

But somehow it seems like families expect the most explanations and are the most judgmental. They tend to make you feel like an outcast, like a stranger, like the black sheep; You might as well be around ignorant authority who don't give you a chance to explain your story, situation or point of view. They just try to shut you up until they get the result they want. The people who are ignorant are only concerned with you becoming a statistic. It doesn't matter if you're a woman or man or child, you are not excluded from racism, racial injustice, prejudice or ignorance. We need to change this.

We have enough social injustices within police brutality, ignorance, racial profiling, bullying, prejudices, stereotyping. . . Black and brown people have been affected by all of these. We share a lot of the same struggles. We hurt, we suffer. We need to understand each other's struggles and we need to support each other, especially when death is too often the outcome of ignorance. It's beyond wrong when racial profiling takes precedence over wrong and right. But because you may be the color or shade that someone has been taught to dislike or hate, you automatically become the target. I cannot wrap my head around that thought. How is that fair? In what world is that fair? How can we shelter our youth from these inevitable situations? How can we prepare them for having guns pointed at them, being shot at, for simply walking down the street in their own neighborhood or driving to school or work in their own car, or simply sleeping in their own bed in their own home? These are everyday actions that you must do to live life, get to work, function in society. How can we protect our youth and ourselves? What is it going to take to change this? How do we protect our human rights? Our children are witnessing our people being murdered in broad daylight as they beg for their lives and yet still nothing is being done to correct this. How do we explain to them that those not of our color or shade see us as less valuable while we are constantly teaching them that we are kings and queens? We must teach **all** that the equality that is supposed to exist, MUST exist. As much as we hate to have the sit down talk with our black and brown babies about how dangerous the world is for them. . . We must educate our youth because those not of our color feel entitled. They are determined to strip us of any known bloodlines we have knowledge of in an attempt to make us feel less worthy or undervalued. I know one thing. Our youth needs to understand that this is not a thing of the past. The climate of expressed hate and racism has been progressing and it's at an all-time high. We cannot allow them to go out in the world and be naive. We cannot allow lack of knowledge to lead them into becoming another forgotten name or another name added to the obituaries. We need our youth to understand the power they possess and use it for positivity, for change.

Twelve

Nightmares haunt
Her in the sunlight
Memories taunt
her sleep at night
But she's only twelve
Only twelve
Visions of blood
Hurt and pain
Tears flood
Her eyes, heavy rain
She's mad all the time
But doesn't know why
She fights anger
Yet she's terrified
But she's only twelve
Only twelve
She doesn't understand

Emotional roller coaster
Getting out of hand
Needing closure
But all she sees
Is her hero fallen
All she can do is freeze
She just wants normalcy again
But she's only twelve
Only twelve
She can't remember
How that feels
Constant reminders
Seem to steal
Her childhood away
Lost in her own mind
Nothing anyone can say
Until she's ready to leave it all behind
But she's only twelve
She's only twelve.

Wrongfully Accused

Clearly dismissed
My pregnancy
Cold metal gripped my wrists
Sat me down forcefully
As if an option was to resist
No empathy
Asking questions
Seemed to be wrong
Responded with aggression
Why is this taking so long
And with no discretion
Innocent all along

My anger is fueled
My face slammed on the hood
This is their tool
But didn't react as I could
Kept it cool
As against the black and white I stood
Used words protected her in a way
That made the blues doubt their suspicion

It was foul play
But seemed we fit the description
Of two people who got away
From somewhere we had never been.

Spit

I was so naïve
I couldn't believe
The idea I couldn't conceive
At first I thought
Driving in a Blue hood, Red car
Then I thought how that idea was so bizarre
To be spit at
To be spit on
Like we were some old alley cats
Or a doormat to be walked on
I looked at him in shock
Immediately I drove faster
Didn't stop at the crosswalk
The nerve of that bastard
My friend in the passenger seat
Was as upset as I was on the inside
The Latino guys in the street

Their hate amplified
Shown by their actions as we drove by
A black and brown couple
Automatically disqualified
In their small ignorant bubble
To actually count as people who matter
But our diversity is what helped open doors
To get the YES answers
When people got NO's because of race wars
So tell me how, you spitting at me
Helps your situation in life
It doesn't get you a job or degree
Or get you into heaven in the afterlife
But what I drove away with that day
Was more than priceless
My eyes were now open to a world I never knew
My voice will no longer be silenced
Because this is something no one should get used to.

Moonlight Blues

I gave him everything he asked for
Humbly did as I was told
Reluctant to turn my head towards my door
Since he was on the opposite side, attitude cold

No reason for us to be stopped
No reason for standing on the passenger side
But is there any good reason for a racist cop?
At this point praying no one dies

Red and blue lights still flash, spotlight in our face
Still he asked the passenger for identification
Only because of his race
No scale to measure my frustration

What did we do wrong?
No crime did we commit
I don't want to be a repeat of a song
The song where the cop loses it

Shoots and kills someone innocent
Because of hate they claim never existed
And they are just using their gun as an instrument
A tool to protect and serve because he'll say we resisted

The whole time we hide the fear
Not fear of a man
But fear of not living past this day in this year
While his gun pointed, we sit, he stands

All we were doing was driving home together
Two people building a bond that night
Now under this unjustified pressure
Can't even enjoy a drive under the moonlight.

With No Disrespect

As I walk up the stairs
I hear her raspy voice
She gives no fucks or cares
That I was his choice
She was this Louisiana voodoo witch
Who liked to try to hurt my feelings
I was referred to as the Mexican Bitch
To her so unappealing
But I wasn't in the relationship for her
It was her son I loved
So up the stairs, the pot to stir
With my Latina presence I rubbed
All in her face, just miserable
She stared with such hatred
But this made her vulnerable
I chose to love, her space I invaded
With a charming smile

She hated every minute
But I loved her all the while
Nothing about my love was counterfeit
But still her heart stone cold
So I finally got the courage
To say, "I won't let you control
The way I feel or let you discourage
My love from giving his all.
I don't need your approval
Nor your blessing. This isn't protocol
I'd usually show respect but your approval
I no longer seek. His love is
Everything I need. You now mean nothing.
He is mine and I am his,
And we will continue to live our lives loving.
We rebuke your hate and utilize
The energy to make us stronger
So with no disrespect, we will rise
Thanks to your hate fueling us to last longer."

This War

At first I had no words,
Just instant rage
No understanding towards
The negligence on this world's stage
A puppet show in which
Someone used the innocent
Continuing to destroy the already broken bridge
When so easily it could have been prevent-
Ed. . . heartless souls ensure
That racism lives but I refuse
To sneak out the back door
Someone must assume responsibility.
A boycott of the company is not enough
This disgusting display
This racist act
Don't you dare downplay
And, NO! I am not overreact-
Ing. . .I won't stand for ignorance
I am a mother, a protector,
I want to make a difference
I will continue to love
With my Kolorblind Soul
Until we can get rid of
Racism and we are whole
I may die before this war is won
But knowledge I will continue to feed
Even if I have to do it one by one
In order to overcome and succeed.

Our Youth

They are dying, depressed
They are hungry, neglected
With no cuffs under arrest
This is life through their prospective

But yet they still love wholeheartedly
Like you did no wrong
No hate do they feel or see
They are immensely strong.

They are not racist until taught
That skin color makes a difference
For love they have fought
But all they get is ignorance

I know that my struggle
Is worth every tear
Teaching them to be humble
And there's only God to fear

My children are everything
So I just don't understand
How you wouldn't give anything
To make sure their future is grand

The innocence they possess
The love they give
Why would you want to repress
Their aspiration to live

Let your children learn and play
Don't let them grow up too fast
Cherish them before one day
Their childhood is just their past.

Didn't Know

I didn't know
I was so naïve
To even think
Or believe
That you wouldn't judge
That you would treat me
Like a human being
That you would treat me
Like you see me as equal
That you would treat me
Like I did something wrong
For just simply being me.

Trying To Understand

I'm soul-searching trying to understand
You know what it feels like first hand
To be discriminated against
You were once the oppressed
Screaming for love, fighting for equality
Against prejudice's monstrosity

I'm soul-searching trying to understand
When exactly you began
To think that you are held at a higher regard
In this society that tries so hard
To belittle the black and brown
To keep us down
Keep us from rising to the top
This needs to stop
And even though you agree
Still somehow you don't see
Your own prejudices and racism push through
Is there anything anyone can do
To make you see
That you are not like me

I'm soul-searching trying to understand
What I do understand
I take heed and remain humble
I acknowledge my ancestry and the struggle
So I empathize with others
When will you discover
You're not the only one that had a hard life
You made it through despite
The obstacles you overcame
But that still gives you no right to claim
That you are superior
It really makes you mentally inferior
By being too stubborn to open your mind
Get to know the humankind
As individual people should be your goal
Then you can be proud of being a colorblind soul.

Silent But Deadly

Everyone notices
The smell so strong
But they pretend
Like nothing's wrong

All smiles in the room
Laughs and talk
But the stench is suffocating
In their path I won't walk

I don't want to smell
The guilty stench
Of silent jokes in their head
Thirst your quench

For the remarks unsaid
Feed the fire
To keep the spark alive
While in your head you conspire

I don't hate anyone
But I hate you
Because your fake
And deceive to be true

You're trying too hard
To prove something false
But your fakeness
In your dark thoughts

Will come out to the light
And show your permanent residence
Choosing left over right
Continuing to choose ignorance.

Cold World

I can't handle this hate!
My kids are growing up in this mess!
It shouldn't be their fate,
Their freedom being repossessed.
How can they become great?
How can they achieve success
When injustice is all that is demonstrate
-ed? I will not allow them to settle for less.
I have taught my kids love and being fair
So they can't understand why race
Is causing common warfare.
To me it's such a disgrace
That I have to explain this chaos,
This race war, this inequality.
Cold world when the majority of innocence lost
Is taken by unlawful authority.
And no, two wrongs don't make a right,
But tell me, would there even be a fight
If the bad ones just demonstrated self-control
Or better yet be taught to be a colorblind soul?

ethnicity

noun
1. the fact or state of belonging to a social group that has a common national or cultural tradition.

difference

noun
1. a point or way in which people or things are not the same.

Many times. . .

our youth and even some adults have a hard time being accepted because people are constantly pointing out their differences in a negative manner. They are not treated the same due to their different ethnicities or physical attributes. These are things that are part of who they are and yes, their attributes contribute to their individuality, but their attributes do not define them as a human. They are not who they are ONLY because of their ethnicity, their skin tone, their hair texture, their body shape. . . They are ALSO who they are because of who they are within. We need to encourage those who are not so confident in themselves because of the rejection they have experienced, to be confident and acknowledge the things about themselves that they are proud of. Especially when the rejection is stemmed from racial issues. We need to teach them to embrace their differences, be proud of who they are and where they come from and to accept others who are different from them. All humans have something to contribute to this world no matter how big or small, what ethnicity or upbringing. We can all greatly benefit from being exposed to different cultures. We can learn from one another by embracing without judgement.

Barbers

Mama, they just didn't cut it right
I sat in the chair
Still. . . like they ask
It just isn't fair
Is it that hard
I mean they go to school
To learn this right
Am I the fool
For expecting more
I'm mixed, I have different sized curls
My hair is not too thick
Gets on my nerves
Don't even want to take a pic
They don't know how to fade
They don't line it up right
They still get paid
Even though my hair didnt come out right
They cut my curls to low
My faux hawk is messed up
I can't just let this go
I will not give up
I have nothing against these barbers
They just aren't the ones for my hair
So Mama, tell me is it fair
To want a barber to do the task
I want a black barber. . . Is that too much to ask?

Correct This

What happened to the days where
We said hello when we passed by
You know back in the days where
You didn't have to try
To be nice to another
You supported your folks
Helped out a sister or brother
Encouraged each other's dreams and hopes
Now all guards are up permanently
Racism running wild
Doing damage remorselessly
And the main one who smiled
Right in your face
Is the same Mutha sucka
Against you in a race
But you still end up the winner
But really who wants to live like this
When will this be corrected
Yes, we can sit and reminisce
But we need to stop acting disconnected
And learn to appreciate
The culture of us as a whole
Respect each other and create
A way to reach all goals
To better you individually
Which betters us as one
Support each other unconditionally
Every night til the rising of the last sun.

guilty

adjective
1. having committed an offense, crime, violation, or wrong, especially against moral or penal law; justly subject to a certain accusation or penalty;

association

noun
1. a mental connection between ideas or things.
2. a connection or cooperative link between people or organizations.

It's extremely difficult to express...

the worries and anxieties that you have as a parent. But it's even more difficult to express the fear that comes along with those worries and anxieties when you're raising a black or brown child. The conversations that you must have with them to open their eyes and taint their innocence are heartbreaking. But these conversations must be had, in hopes that they can comprehend that the negativity of some people in this world, can possibly end their lives. The way they are viewed by unlawful authority can place them in a position to alter the rest of their life in such a negative way. We cannot control those people who will view them as guilty just because of the company they keep or who they are company to. And although the negativity isn't what we as parents like to focus on, our youth cannot go out into this world unaware of the impact that it can have on them. They need to understand that racial injustice, racism, prejudice, ignorance all exist. As hurtful as it is, we wish that we did not have to have these conversations. But we try as parents to provide helpful solutions, possible outcomes, scenarios to play out and we pray for the best. We try to instill in our children to stand strong and never allow anyone to hurt them, but unfortunately, sometimes these are the things that get them hurt by the people we have warned them about. The balance is difficult because we cannot control the actions or thoughts of others who see us as an enemy, threat, or simply not as entitled as them. Our children coming home, us coming home, and safely, is never guaranteed. So when you are having these conversations, whether you're the parent or child, listen to each other. Be open. Talk. Communicate. What one another may say, just might save your life. We have to save each other. No one else will.

Guilty By Association

Sour is the taste of rejection
Look at me, don't you see your reflection
Why is it you can't show me any affection?
To that I have an objection
The affection I endure is discrimination
I guess I'm guilty by association
But what am I guilty of
Guilty because of whom I love
Again, what am I guilty of?
I hoped it was something you could rise above
But apparently conditional is your love
It's like I've been crucified
My family's love I've been deprived
And many tears my soul has cried
And through the pain a little of me died
Your joy of revenge equals my pain
That's how I know you're a little insane
But when you cannot stop the rain
Remember these words I write
And maybe clear will be your sight
And you'll realize that
Sour is the taste of rejection
Look at me, don't you see your reflection
Why is it you can't show me any affection?
To that I have an objection
The affection I endure is discrimination
I guess I'm guilty by association.

That One Day

Sad and scary truths
About being a parent
To a young black king
Anything can happen, anything.
One day he may not return home
Because of the justice system.
One day he may not return home
No matter what our household income.
One day he may not return home
Because of the hate you teach your children.
One day he may not return home
Because you view him as a villain.
One day he may not return home
Just because of his skin color.
One day he may not return home
Because he defended himself from a racial slur.

One day he may not return home
And he'll never meet his future wife.
One day he may not return home
Even after begging for his life.
One day he may not return home
Because those who were supposed to protect and serve
Kill him in broad daylight.
One day he may not return home.
Will that be the day you realize
This isn't right?
I can't keep him sheltered inside
Although I wish I could protect him forever.
And no amount of tears a parent has cried
Will ever truly measure
The worry we carry everyday
And we pray that we will never see
That One Day.

Part Two
Love and Empathy

I Can Only Be Me

I don't know why I hide
all my feelings deep inside
but just the thought of losing you
I don't know what I would do
we haven't spoken in so long
I know that this is wrong
but do you really hate me
because I wanted to be free
but I gave all I could
I did everything I thought I should
that's why I'm so surprised
that I'm being penalized
for wanting to be free
for wanting to be me.

spiritual

adjective
1. relating to or affecting the human spirit or soul as opposed to material or physical things

divine

adjective
1. of, from, or like God or a god.

connection

noun
1. a relationship in which a person, thing, or idea is linked or associated closely with something or someone else.

oss

(origin Brazilian Jiu jitsu)
1. persevering when pushed
2. manifestation of KI energy
3. slang response meaning understood

When you connect with someone...

especially spiritually, in a way that you've never connected with anyone before, it's like... it's like magic. It's like magic with fireworks on a dark, clear, starry night with a cool breeze where your connection shines brighter than the lights from the city by the sea where the water reflects the moon. You become one in a sense. You have an intense sense of understanding and empathy. This type of connection is sent from God. It's unexplainable. Connecting with someone in such a divine way is an experience so few share. You can't fake it or ignore it. It exists and your soul yearns for communication. It has no prejudice, no color, no discriminations or preferences. It is simply a soul connection that is almost as strong as love. Far and few in between get to experience this oneness with another soul, but when you feel it, nothing else can replace it.

Me And Mal

Nickerson Gardens, parked
Exhausted, overworked
Waiting on Mal
Down for the long haul
In the glove, got the strap
But tired as I was I had to nap
I used to fall asleep in my CRX,
All alone, a Mexican girl in projects.
Never did I fret or frown
Because I knew Mal was somewhere around
He'd get mad that I fell asleep
Because he knew I had the heat
But no matter what, I was protected.
God put me there, I was selected.
Back and forth on the 710 Freeway
Us, singing and rapping, our voices on replay
No radio in the CRX anyway,
But fun was on our agenda every day
Writing songs by the water
Building together, friendship stronger
Ups and downs
But we adjusted our crowns
Always picking each other up
Now that we've grown up
He's still a little insane
But I wouldn't have it any other way. . .
It's good to reminisce of good times passed.
It's how I knew our friendship would last.

U.B. OSS

You provide perception
Beyond ordinary sight
I see the potential
Feel the hunger, appetite
I can see our energy
No light shines this bright
Only one in tune
My third eye
Medicate while I meditate
Intuitive foresight
I can hear you calling out
Spiritual sound bite
Feel the lunar energy
Whenever we reunite
Protect you at all costs
Just give me the green light
Ability to see through the façade
No oversight
Expressing creativity
My fire you ignite
Higher consciousness
Don't be scared, just sit tight
Discover value in our lessons
Supreme insight
We are the ones
Magnetic, we unite.

side

verb
1. support or oppose in a conflict, dispute, or debate

represent

verb
1. state or point out (something) clearly

In your community,

in society, I believe there are two sides of this human revolution: Discrimination & Prejudice and Love & Empathy. What revolution does your soul belong to? What is it that you represent? What is it that you stand for? Do you even choose a side? Do you stand for what is morally right or do you just go with the flow of things in order to not stir things up? Do you stand in silence as compliance to avoid confrontation?

So many people need to learn that you need to stand for something and be true to it. Stand up for what's right and make sure you are fighting for causes that mean something to this world, that will make a positive change. Don't allow others to change the world without your consent. Make a difference in this world, whether it's in your home, your community, your city. . . Represent something positive. Choose to be significant. Be a leader in our community. Become a strong presence in this world. Be a moving force in our revolution.

Paving The Way

You enjoy today
But they paved the way
You live in the suburbs
Pay no mind to the past
Saying they don't deserve
A thing or pain doesn't last
Raped, beaten, dethroned
Hung from trees
Not property but somehow owned
Given foreign disease
This history is worth so much more
Than the reparations offered
You choose to ignore
That they have suffered
No amount is enough
To heal broken hearts
But you continue to handcuff
Continue to try to break apart
A village so strong
Invading lives
Killing the men
And raping their wives

You feel good creating programs
Supposed to be a stepping stone
Fuck Uncle Sam
Give back the throne
How much is enough pain
How much is to be endured
You expect to not hear complaints
And you try to shut down every entrepreneur
Can you afford the reparations due?
No amount is enough in my eyes
You exploit every avenue
Take credit as you capitalize
On contributions made
While their names blow in the wind
Making sure their history fades
Because to see anyone else win
Would diminish everything you stand for
But miseducation
Has caused hate and rage against
Any sort of reparation
While you hide behind
The big elephant in every room
Using handcuffs and bars to confine
Using the courtroom
As your weapon when

The bullets don't hit
But still you can't understand the anger
That slavery still exists
How long will it take
To get what is due after so long
No memory will be erased
The fight against wrong
Will always be fought in this nation
Until you pay compensation
On dues owed for slavery and segregation
When will you pay the reparations?
When everything falls apart and is broken?
When hatred prevents you from enjoying YOUR day?
Will you then give back everything you've stolen
Or will you simple mindedly place blame for paving the way?

Sides

Battling
                                                Battling

Fighting
                                                Fighting

Confronting
                                                Securing

Targeting
                                                Defending

Opposing
                                                Upholding

Hating
                                                Protecting

Are you on the outside
Or the inside?
With what side
Do you ride?
Do you pick a side
Or go run and hide?
Will this subside
So we can rise?
Or continue to be pushed aside
Unjustified?
We will no longer back slide
Or allow anyone to divide.
We will continue to be dignified
And won't allow you to destroy our pride.

Targets

All the kids play together
Basketball, handball, video games
Their friendship isn't measured
By society's strains
Until they become teenagers
Skin color plays a role
Best friends become strangers
It's wrong, we all know
But nothing is done to prevent
This, it's like its accepted
But so much of my life has been spent
Being disconnected and dissected
Because I do not judge
I love all of our differences
But many have held a grudge
Against me. They can't understand the significance
They display their ignorance through rejection
But how can you enforce your racism
On kids with such hostile aggression
And still expect them to overcome
Creating negativity
You make them targets of hate
When they should be able to be free
Reach their goals and be great.

Chains

It breaks my heart into pieces
When my children ask me
For invisible nonexistent adhesive
To fix a hurt I cannot see
I don't know how deep it cut
Or if it will leave a scar
I just go with my gut
And ask God in prayer
To heal this brand new pain
They don't understand why
And they want me to explain
Why they are being identified
As "bad" by peers because they are different
My beautiful melanin babies
Don't allow the ignorance
To weigh too heavy
You are as special as they come
You are cultured in a way
They can never become
So believe in love and continue to pray
You're phenomenal chosen royalty
They may say you don't fit in now
But that's the cruelty of society

Remember they can only hurt your feelings if you allow
So be strong and be proud of who you are
Reach your goals be unstoppable
But be compassionate it will take you far
You were made to be phenomenal
With these loving words
I hope to protect you and give strength
Keep you on the right path towards
Breaking societies racists chains.

Given, Token

In the looks that are given
In the actions that are taken
I'm torn between being not Latina enough
Because my Spanish is broken
From both sides it's rough
The hate is constantly spoken
The other side is that I am too ethnic
What the fuck does that even mean
I'm told a side I must pick
I'm not American enough so I'm called a beaner... but I'm not pale enough to
Fit in or play nice with those
Lighter than my shade. what am I to do?
I will continue being me I suppose
They tell me stick with my kind
But I firmly believe we are one
So in every shade I seem to find
A similarity, something that I can understand empathy is a gift
That I have been chosen to give to this world
From their energy I get lifted... a kind of love has occurred
Even when they hate
Love I chose to create
From the looks that are given
And from the actions that are taken.

Ambiguous

If you can't tell my ethnicity
By looking at me,
Then the only
Thing you need to know is me...
Not where my family is from
Or where I grew up.
What is the outcome?
So you can cover up
The racist remarks
Or refrain from making them
Don't let me unarm
That gun, continue to condemn
Me for the ambiguity
Of my appearance
Decide how racist you'll be
I'm giving you clearance
Because I don't want fake
I don't want ignorance
None of your words will break
Me or make a difference
On what moves I make
Or what I believe
But for your own sake
Just know... Me... you will never defeat.

strength

noun
1. the quality or state of being strong, in particular.
2. the emotional or mental qualities necessary in dealing with situations or events that are distressing or difficult.

overcome

verb
1. succeed in dealing with (a problem or difficulty)

In dealing with racism, prejudice and ignorance,

it takes a lot from you mentally, emotionally and spiritually to stay strong in your position and do what you believe to be right. A lot of leaders and people who take on leadership roles all have one thing in common: strength and resilience to overcome. The more you go through and overcome a difficult situation, the stronger you become. Lots of people say it's not how many times you fall, but it's how many times you get back up that counts. I also believe that what you do to continue on stronger than before makes a huge impact on those around you who you may not even realize are watching. Your journey, your story may inspire someone to do something they never had enough courage to do on their own. Strength comes in different forms. You can use it in our own life and you can use it to encourage others to better their lives. Acceptance and forgiveness also play huge roles in strength and overcoming. Acceptance is important because you must accept that there will be obstacles in order to face them with tenacity and perseverance. Sometimes you must have the strength to forgive someone who isn't sorry. Sometimes you have to forgive someone who you will never get an apology from.

Forgiveness is important because holding onto something negative reflects in all you do whether you realize the effects of it or not. Sometimes it can cause bitterness or a negative outlook on future situations. Strength is not always something that can be taught. Sometimes you must go through difficult situations in order to learn. However, understand that you must listen to those who have come before you and faced similar obstacles. Learn what was beneficial and learn how to improve the plan in order to overcome and become more successful. Mental, emotional and spiritual strength are the most powerful things to possess. You can accomplish and overcome anything with mental, emotional and spiritual strength.

Stronger Than You

Mental quarantine
Because there's no physical escape
Or any vaccine
You are such a disgrace
To even have such a thought
Yet you create illusions
That you have not fought
Against your flesh and blood human
Pretending there's no difference
In the way you treat one
It's purely ignorance
But your war is not won
By either side
Although I'll allow you to claim the battle
Because you no longer have to hide.
While this wild racist horse I straddle
With a firm grip
For the ride of my life,
I will not allow you to rip
Me apart because of your hateful strife.

Stand Proud

Every morning, I open my eyes
I pray that God protects my son
I don't want to end up a mother who cries
Because racism has won.
I never knew it would be this hard
Addressing the injustices our young men face
Never letting down their guard
All because of their race.
It's hard to watch the brutality
So unbelievable that this is our life
Higher and higher rates of mortality
Because of this endless strife.
But my son has it double time
Not knowing where he fits in
Society has him working overtime
To feel whole within
I have taught him that he is strong
They will never take his crown.
Stand tall Son, it's never wrong
To be proud of being Black and Brown.

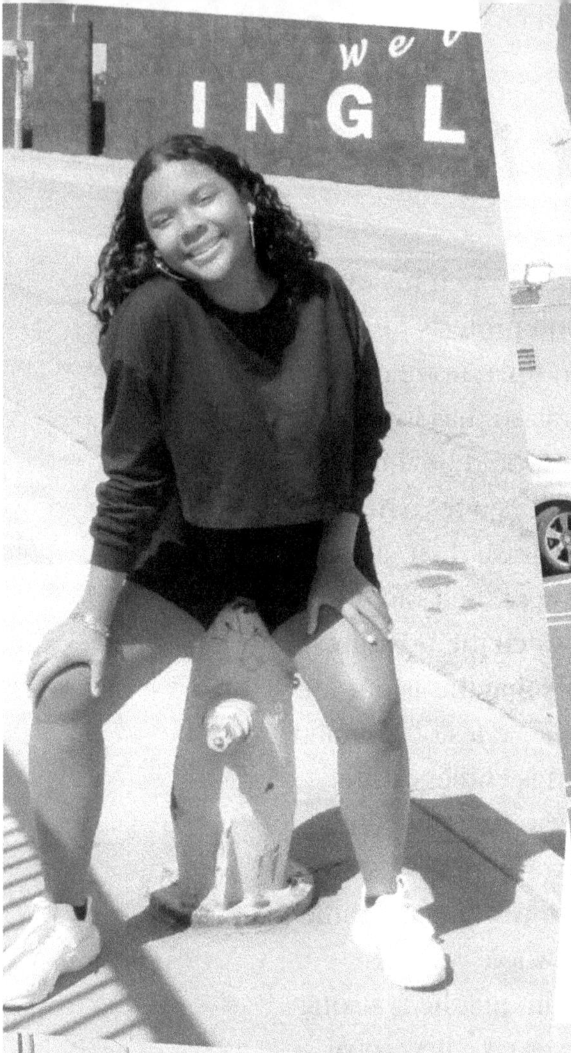

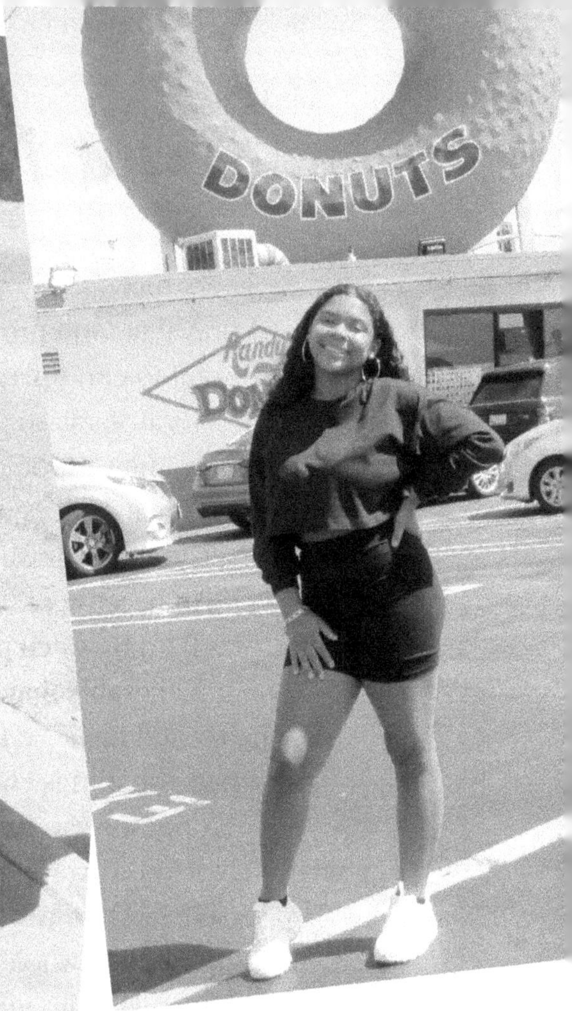

DONUTS

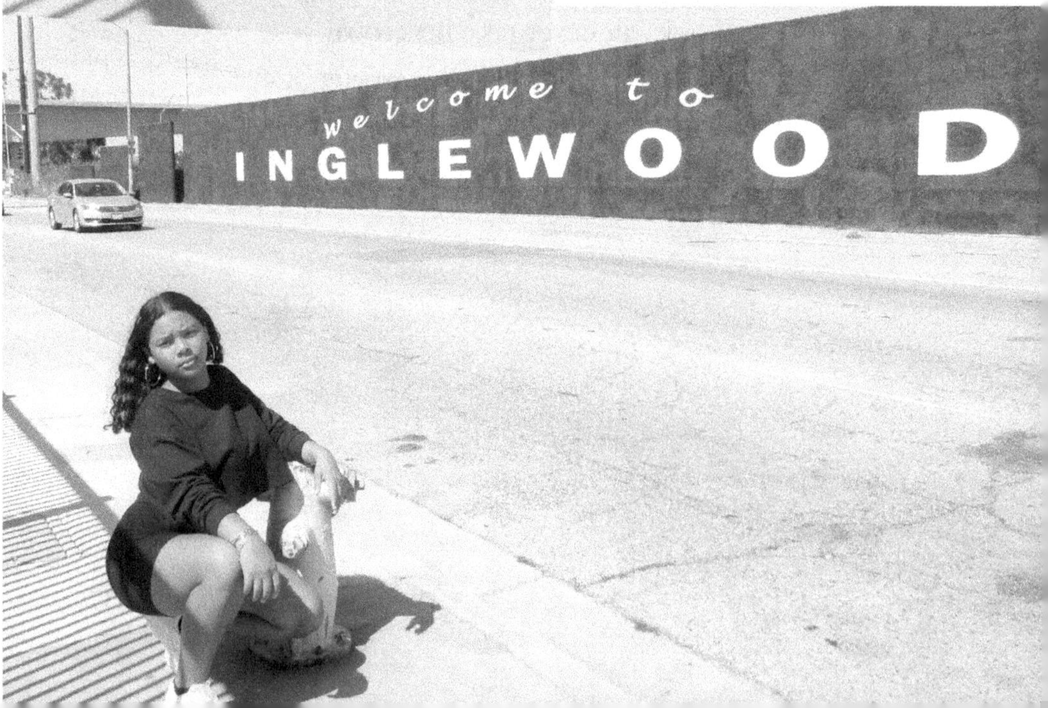

welcome to
INGLEWOOD

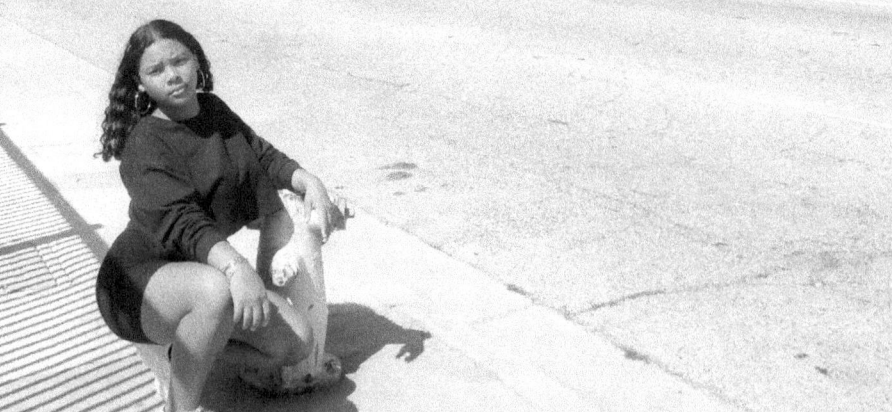

I Love Me

The stares
Hard glares
Talk about my hair
Curly but I'm fair
or light skinned,
who cares
It's unfair
They try to make me feel
Like I'm not real
They want me to fix
The fact that I'm mixed
But I won't let their envy
Cause me insecurity
These beautiful lips,
Curvy hips
Causing conflicts
They will never make me feel
Like I'm not real
I've been taught to be strong
Admit when I'm wrong
Never judge by appearance
Tenacity and perseverance
I am human
I am a woman
They will never make me feel
Like I'm not real.

Enlightenment

Fully comprehend
The situation at hand
Becoming spiritually aware
Self-knowledge and self-care
Valuing the worth of individualism
Without dismissing existence of racism
Education is key to prevention
It's truly important to make a human connection
Wisdom is nothing without
Courage to reach out.
So enlighten your soul
To knowledge grab a hold
Society will leave you dying and bleeding
If you do not exercise reason.
Stand strong to face
Betterment for the human race.

love

noun
1. an intense feeling of deep affection

embrace

verb
1. accept or support (a belief, theory, or change) willingly and enthusiastically

Love is one of the most...

intense, overwhelming and deepest feelings you can feel. I have always believed and still do believe that love has no boundaries, no prejudice, no limits, no restrictions. I have been shown love in many relationships whether they were romantic, friendships or family. There have been some people who have embraced me no matter what, unconditionally. Embracing others, no matter what ethnicity, background, situation, culture or differences, is one of the keys to creating a better environment for us to live in. Expressing empathy and unconditional love is exactly what we need to show one another including, strangers and neighbors in order to attempt to end racism. This type of genuine love is the miracle that has the potential to restore humanity. In our revolution, we must embrace and love each other. Be a Kolorblind Soul.

Colorblind Love

I tell him I love him
He says he loves me in return
When the lights dim
Or the candles burn
We light the room
With the sparks that fly
His essence I consume
Our soul connection magnifies
I tell him he's like magic
the way his skin is one with mine
he says it's all romantic
I knock him out like moonshine
He says his magic is his melanin
And his charismatic allure
I say he's my magic medicine
Lucky to find a love so pure
His voice baritone
His dark smooth skin
He feels like home
Always will, always has been
It could be his curly hair
Or his loving brown eyes
No one can compare
I'm his love and he's mine.

Treasure

The vibration of your voice
Sends chills up my spine
As your sweet melodies
Tell me you're mine
Planning the future
So much in store
Pulling my waist close
My body you explore
Love harmonizing
Never missing a beat
You know what I like
Your kisses so sweet
With candles burning
Sativa in the air
Our bodies' beautiful music
A love we both share
Lyrics of treasures
Only time will reveal
No matter how it appears
We both know this is real

Love Hazard

Fighting my guard
Inner battle, struggle
He's making it hard
Not to want to be a couple
But will he break my heart
I don't think I can handle it
I can't handle falling apart
So I'm hesitant to commit
Trying to give this the benefit of the doubt
Don't want to think about
How I thought this time was different
But somehow it still didn't
Work out
No I don't think I can live without
Him, and it's hard to think about
So for now let's just hangout
No expectation
No disappointment
Hard to be patient
When I'm full of excitement
Every interaction
Immediate attraction
Constant satisfaction
No distractions

A Magnetic Force Occurs
From the minute we lock eyes
A charismatic hazard
Was love in disguise
An energy exchange
Showering with affection
I cannot contain
He's nearly perfection
People make movies
About the connection we share
Making love by the sea
He has me floating in air
Our secrets locked in the moonlight
Every touch, every word
Heart beating at the speed of light
Still my vision isn't blurred
Can't seem to come down
From the brightest phase
I wanna drown
In full moon rays
Electricity in the waves

Thunder crashing down
Said I'll never get married
But for him, I might write vows
He loves me generously
Mutual understanding of the complexity
We both possess mentally
Satisfying emotionally and spiritually
Can't express how unique
Our immortal rapport
No words I can speak
Can describe this love evermore
He's the sun, I'm the moon
Infinite eclipse
Totally consumed
Luminous abyss
The ocean's so deep
Don't want him to disappear
Wake up from my sleep
And the man of my dreams is still here.

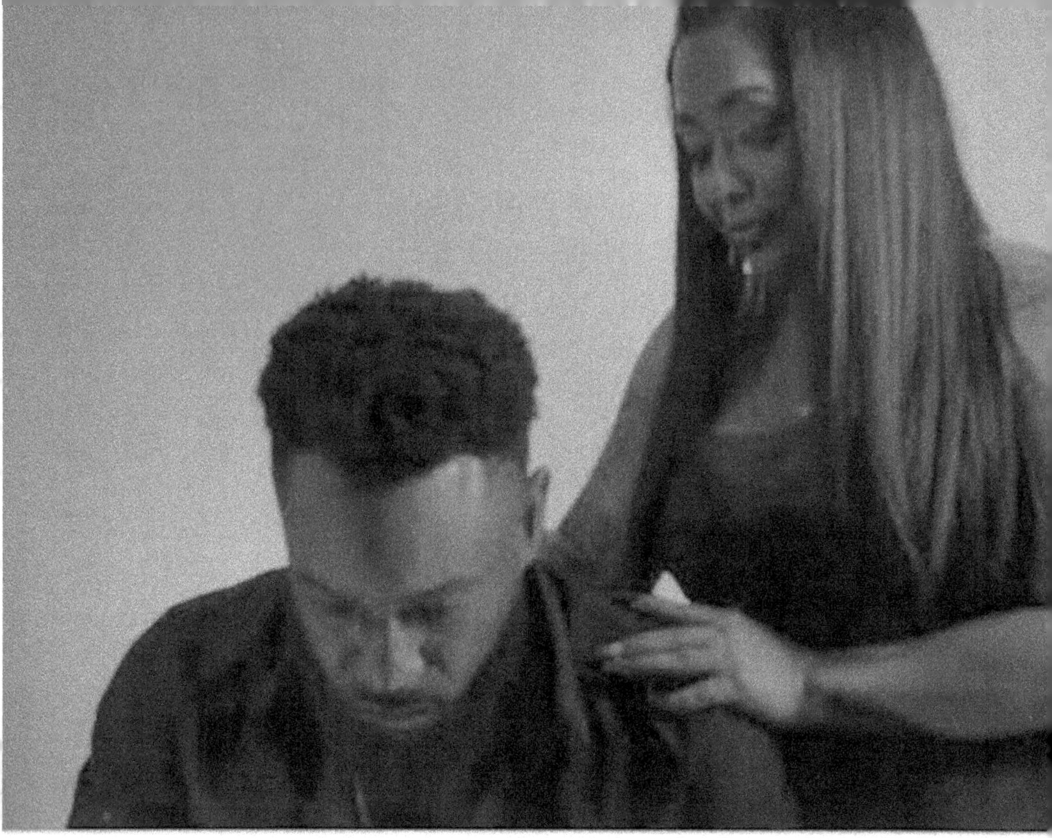

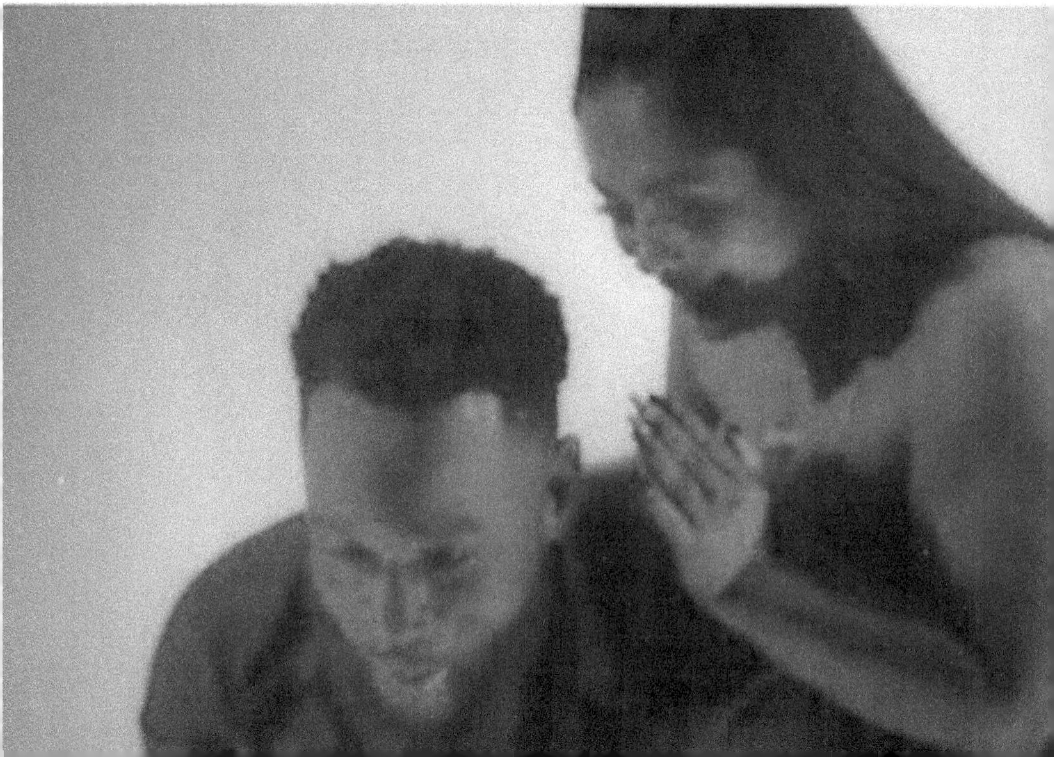

Can't Get Enough

You call me in that voice
Oh that voice
I rush out the door
Can't hold back anymore
I'm out of my mind over you
Got me doing things I never do
Racing on the freeway
Then I walk through your doorway
I sit down and wait
You appear and you captivate
My heart in one look
With admiration you took
One glance at me
Into my soul you could see
You take my hand
Now we stand
Face to face
You hold me in a tight embrace
Your breath on my neck
Takes my breath away
We just connect
Never wanting to stray
Pulling me closer
You kiss my lips
Feel as if we were
A total eclipse
No one else comes close
It's only me and you
Can't get enough to overdose
On the things you do
The excitement I feel
When you smile at me
I know this is real
You set me free.

How I Love You

So madly
Deeply
In love with
The way you love me
The way you look
In my eyes
Before we kiss
You mesmerize
My body
With your energy
Your passion
Such intensity
You penetrate
My inner being
With your magic
Leaving
Me speechless
Fulfilling
With a completeness
That is so willing
To love you in return
So madly, deeply
In love with you
For eternity.

She

inspired by Anita Hise

she told me that I had to toughen up
this world is not forgiving
she taught me how to stay prayed up
I didn't deserve the life I was living
she took me in when my mother didn't
she taught me love and compassion
she had no agenda hidden
just simply to share her vision
she told me it's ok to cry
everyone makes mistakes
she said just flap your wings, you'll fly
progression is key, fly with grace
she believed in me more than I believed in me
I soaked up every minute with her
she shared the knowledge, I so desperately seeked
I've always kept her in my prayers
she never allowed our appearances
to change the love she displayed for me
she reassured me there's no color in perseverance
no color did her love ever see.

Forever Reflected

I never knew a love so deep was possible
I never knew the pain inside would fade
I never knew my body was capable
I never knew I could feel so afraid
This love I feel in incredible
Somehow it melted the pain away
My mind is on a whole new level
I thank GOD for him everyday
Even though he can't wipe away my tears
He makes me smile endlessly
He seems to take away all my fears
And place pride inside me
I listen to him breathe at night
While he sleeps so peacefully
I dream of all the things that might
Come about and things meant to be
No replacement will I find ever
Unexplainable it will remain
This love I will feel forever
Whether my days are sunny or filled with rain
He gives me so much more than expected
And it's only just begun
My love will forever be reflected
In my precious first born son.

My Little Girl

I always wanted boys
So I could buy Tonka toys
So they could be Mommy's boys
And all day and night make noise
But I went to the doctor
Second time around
These cute little body parts were hers...
Hers? Silence was the sound.
Joy and pain entered my heart
Joy because she'd be a little me
Pain because I didn't know where to start
To a daughter, what kind of mother would I be?

I heard her cry
My little butterfly
I took a big sigh
Then I began to cry
Once I held her
I was no longer scared
With all my heart I loved her
There was a bond we shared.
I told her not worry
That I would love her forever
It would be an adventurous journey
And I'd be by her side through whatever
I knew it would be okay
When she looked up at me
If I continue to pray
The greatest mom to a little girl I'll be.

Early Bird

Do you remember the words
Every day I would sing
Three little birds. . .
Don't worry 'bout a thing. . .
Rubbing my belly
Waiting to see you fly
It hit hard though, reality
One morning in July
Was just the beginning of a long road
Two weeks hospitalized seems like eight
A new burden on me now bestowed
Patience and strength I had to demonstrate
You'd come soon
Six weeks early
Three in the afternoon
Such a tiny thing, hair so curly
My third little bird
Ready for the world
So mighty and strong
My precious four pound girl
They told me your chances
Were good but not great
I knew these circumstances
Would only elevate
Determination to live
So love again will win
So my early bird
Spread your wings
Fly together, three little birds
Don't worry 'bout a thing. . .

empathy

noun
1. the ability to understand and share the feelings of another.

legacy

noun
1. a thing handed down by a predecessor

impact

noun
1. the action of one object coming forcibly into contact with another

Empathy is...

important to sustain a relationship of any kind when dealing with other people no matter the situation. Situations sometimes arise when you are put in a position to see things from another perspective. Learn to appreciate those situations because from those moments, there's a lesson to be learned. So make it a point to always try to take a step back from the obstructed view and see things from the outside looking in, see the bigger picture. Stand up for what you believe to be right, but remember to take others into consideration while doing it. Figure out what you are supposed to take from the situation and how you can improve your life or the lives of the people around you. Sometimes you have to let others pull your soul strings to make you feel what they feel or make you feel something that you've never felt before. Being empathetic leaves a lifetime imprint on someone's heart, someone's life. It may inspire them to become a better person or want to do better for others. Empathy has the capability to inspire others to leave an impactful, lasting legacy.

In this lifetime, what are you doing to create a legacy to leave for future generations? What is it that you are doing to leave an impact on others? I have figured out that my mission is to leave a legacy of love, a Kolorblind Soul Love. I've been through the ups and downs as I'm sure you have too. Everyone's journey is not the same. But through my eyes and the things that I have seen and felt, I believe that it is my moral duty to carry this message and deliver it to as many people as possible. I want to encourage you to embrace others' cultures, discover new things while making new friends with different ethnic backgrounds. I encourage you to love people who may need guidance no matter what their past is. Encourage others to follow their dreams. Dream big. Nurture your dream and believe in it with all your heart. Be Great. Be the best version of you possible. No one will ever have as much faith in your dream as you. So never allow your possibility of success or happiness to be controlled by anyone else. And always remember to find beauty in all situations, including your own journey. Don't judge others by their appearance. And most importantly, love and embrace one another without any limitation of learned biases concerning race, ethnicity, skin color, social or economic status.

Let Me

Wanna jump in
Save you from drowning
Just jump in
Cause I can feel your heart pounding
I feel it about to break
Pain shows in eye puddles
Just wanna make
You not feel the struggle
Pour your heart in my hands
Let me show you a love never seen
Tall it stands
No smokescreen
Genuine empathy
Soul healing
Intentionally comforting
Saving your heart from
The anger and hurt
Beating the drum
Healing giving a cure
To a bleeding heart
Growth must occur
An unfortunate new start
But I whisper
In sync with your energy
Reaching a healing connection
To the highest degree
Creating ascension.

We Matter

We can't just leave him there
This couldn't have been an accident
He's bleeding from everywhere
Puddles of blood on the cement
Into space he stares
We can't wait for his consent
Help him now
Call nine one one
Don't know how
Or with what gun
But this is foul
He's someone's son

Don't close your eyes baby
You'll be just fine
Look at me, can you see me
Please don't flat line
This isn't how it's supposed to be
You will not be defined
By this circumstance
Where you weren't wrong
This didn't happen by chance
Please pull through, stay strong
We need to take a stance
Let them hear our song

Our children's lives are in danger
Aimed for our kids but glass shattered
Causing them to scatter
But the bullet was faster
Now we're left with no answers
As we protest "Black Lives Matter".

Soul Strings

His hands so strong yet so gentle
so soft yet so firm
as peaceful as an instrumental
orchestra in sonata form
his wrist movements so smooth
caressing my heart with his fingers
gliding his arms, every move
a gentle whisper
that only I can feel
he gently pulls my soul strings
so I can let people know it's real
This Kolorblind Soul love I bring
from the heavens to teach
that you shouldn't judge
so please do not try to besiege
because I refuse to budge.
this message of love I share
came from a void in my soul
but this was his plan to prepare
me to be a Kolorblind Soul.

Fingerprints

Dipping my quail pen
While it so gently curves over my hand
Into the bottle of powdered ink now wet
Spilling the ink unplanned
But as I clean up my mess
Ink stains my fingertips
I touch the paper leaving a print
Nevertheless
I study my mistake
I wonder why
There are so many lines
This is used to identify
Separates me from the next
Excludes me from the rest
Little lines so complex
In awe so impressed
I am one of one
Phenomenally me
I fingerprinted the rest of my fingers
Just to see the beauty
Of my individuality
My own thoughts
My own ideas
Savvy, I'm a boss
But I have more than spilled ink
God gave me a vision
Nowadays it seems extreme
Since there's so much division
But whether my prints are in ink or scanned
I'm still me and will continue to stand

For everything I believe in
I have everything planned
I want to spark your brain
To make a change
Permanent like a bloodstain
Energy interchange
Convert negative with love
Acceptance and understanding
I want to see growth
So this vision seed I am planting
I want to touch you
With my fingers full of ink
Massaging my fingerprints
On your brain, causing you to think
Leave fingerprints on others
Different colors and shades
So not one is identified
By just their race
I want to touch your soul strings
Stir up your emotions
Wipe your tears
When you're feeling broken
Rebuild you stronger
With no preconceived notion
Of color or society's meaning
Rid of racist remarks spoken
I want to hear my fingerprints
In the words you speak
Influence others to prevent
Anyone from feeling weak
Walk beside them when they're alone
Hold their hand and be their guide
Until they're no longer scared of the unknown

And able to face the world diversified
I want to see my fingerprints
While others try to wipe them clean
See them on everything you touch
While doing things others before you unseen
I want to smell the ink from my fingerprints
On the souls of those you interact with
Teaching others to express without violence
For society that's a win
I want the ink to soak in
Overwhelm you with empathy
Leave imprints on your heart
To understand others with sincerity
But I need more ink
To touch all these souls
I want to fingerprint
All of the holes
All of your voids
So you can heal from the wounds
from the cruelty
Of society's racist battlegrounds
This is a war
That I'm fighting with ink
Leaving my fingerprints
On the racism ship as it sinks.
I want to touch you
Dripping in ink
Encourage you
To always think
I am one of one
Phenomenally me
So now go fingerprint others
To share your inner beauty.

Acknowledgements

First I have to thank **GOD**, for creating me with such an open minded outlook on life, giving me the gift of being the epitome of resilience and for my God-given talent of using words in such a raw expression but also with such grace and creativity. I have to give God praise and recognition for giving me patience in this process. Although it wasn't as rough as publishing my first book, this was a long process and my patience was definitely tested. But I thank God every day for making me a better writer and allowing me to see things from a broader horizon than I ever have before.

The second acknowledgement is to the preteen and teenagers who live in my home, aka my kids. You push me to make moves and reach goals I never believed to be attainable. I love you beyond words. You test my patience, make me mad, upset me, even sometimes make me cry, even though I try hard not to let you see me. But daily, you teach me unconditional love, resilience, grace, perseverance, understanding, empathy and forgiveness. It's not easy living in a single parent household, but you all pull your weight and help when I need you to. I understand that it is even more difficult when your mother has Rheumatoid Arthritis. We've had a rough time during the process of me being diagnosed and finding the correct dosage and correct medicines, surgeries, chemo. All of which would allow me to live as much of a normal life as possible. If I could change the rough patches we went through and cure myself, I would. I know it hasn't been the easiest road to travel, but trust me, I do my best every day because of you three. You make me work harder and push me to my limits. You are my "Why", my reasons to excel, my reasons to make our lives extraordinary, my reasons to be phenomenal. I love you and I want for each one of you to be great, be extraordinary, be your best version of yourself, always believe in yourself, stand up for yourself and others, dream the biggest dreams ever and never give up on your dreams.

The third person I have to recognize is my best friend "E", Eric. He always encourages me with tough love, to keep doing me, to stay focused and fuck anyone who is stopping me from progressing in life. Sometimes you need that tough love. He is always there to listen to me vent without judgement. Ok, he might judge me a little, but it stays between us and we laugh about it at the end of the day. He nudges me to keep going but is also always there to make me laugh and make things fun when I've had a long or difficult day. He keeps me grounded. He treats me like royalty and protects me when I need him to. I do the same for him. Friends and loyalty are hard to come by but he's definitely a rare breed and I wouldn't give him up for the world.

Rockii, my rock. Another person who keeps me grounded but also pumps me up when I need the hype. She keeps me laughing when tears flood my eyes and continues to love me unconditionally. No matter what the circumstances, you remain by my side and I love you for that. . . more than I could ever express.

My G. . . Dominic. Anything I throw at you, you take it and run with it like you have all the faith in the world in little ol' me. You are one person I can count on to help capture the best version of me through photographs that I am proud to share with the world. Anytime I call, you're there. I appreciate your honesty always and the loyalty I have to you is immeasurable. You support me in every endeavor and cheer me on every step of the way. You are the one person in this world who reassures me that I am on my own timeline and perfection cannot be rushed. None of my projects would be complete without you. I appreciate you!

Yas. . . my secret weapon. You encourage me no matter how big my dreams and unattainable as they may seem. You are always an open door no matter personal or business. You make my life just that much easier knowing I have such a beautiful artistic soul in my corner who believes in me. You have been there with me throughout all of my endeavors and can't wait to explore what else we will conquer together. I love you and will always be here for you no matter what just like you are for me.

I can't forget Susie. . . *My favorite, my soulmate of a friend...* I love you to the depths of the ocean. My soul immediately had a permanent magnetic bond with yours. You forever encourage and inspire me. You see through any of my masks with one look. You read me like I wrote an instruction manual on my feelings. You elevate my spirit and ignite the artistic fire inside of me when you see life's obstacles and everyday grunge trying to dim it. I will forever be grateful for your presence in my life. You trust me with your secrets and I trust you with mine. We share a love for the beach and the freedom it allows our soul to release the negative and intake the positive and beauty. If anyone ever said you can't have a soulmate as a friend, they were absolutely wrong and are missing out on such a deep immeasurable friendship. You will forever be my chosen family.

Lastly, one of the most important and also happens to be one of the most influential and positive role models, that I am proud to say, my children have in their lives. My brother, Matthew. Although he's my younger brother, he definitely is an old soul with a thirst for knowledge and keen aspiration for empowerment of self. I could not have accomplished any of my endeavors without him. He's been a pillar in my foundation, a shoulder to lean on, and an ear to listen and undoubtedly a reliable source for feedback and constructive criticism when I need it the most. But most importantly he was my guide. He led me back to the path where I found my faith again after being so extremely lost. He is always willing to give and guide with a loving yet firm outlook and without fail, everything he touches makes a huge positive impact. Thank you so much. You and your support means more to me than you will ever realize.

And a few honorable mentions of some important people who check in on me now and again, but always seem to be sent by God because you are always right on time:

"Boobie Trap" for networking me with a few key players in my journey, Tiffany from *Don't Forget The Sugar* for all the laughs and memes on the hard days and yes, her cakes are delicious, Paul Miller for encouraging me to "share the deep stuff", Mykestro for encouraging me to expand my subject matter beyond love and relationships, reminding me throughout to remain authentic and to not allow my talent or style be altered by anyone, my poetry fam at *Dim Lights* in Pomona for cheering me on in my most vulnerable moments at open mic, Gabriel Raymond from 24 Plus events for providing a platform for me to perform. Thanks to my graphic designer who brought my book logo idea into fruition, Jovee Edwards. A big thanks to Usolosopher for speaking my name into existence for numerous performing opportunities. Chad, thank you for your support and willingness to be part of my project. AJ Lamor, you came late in the game as I was putting the final details of my book together, but nevertheless a pivotal component. Thank you! Last but definitely not least, My Ace, Roderick. By blessing my presence with his, we created an incredible

energy that was captured so beautifully. We made the colorblind love images a dream come true with our photos. You motivate me to stay strong and continue to lead by example. You support me and encourage me to write and be creative. Your support provides a consistency I need in my free spirited world. You continuously show with both your actions and your words that you have faith in my talent. And, not only do you reassure me of my capabilities during my low points, you encourage me to keep going no matter what. . . who could ask for more? I genuinely appreciate your presence in my life. Forevermore.

Thank you ALL from the depths of my soul.

About The Author

Selena "Poet U.B" Garcia is an American poet, author, and survivor of her past. Raised in Pomona, Selena was introduced early to the growing pains of life, which would become her canvas to blossom as a literary artist. She then emerged as a poet and literary emotionalist after her impassioned journey moving and finding her path from Pomona to Inglewood, CA. In 2015, Selena launched her imprint, Poet U.B., an acronym for Poet Urban Butterflii - the apt description of her journey and work. In all her work, the author poet gives readers an intimate, honest point of view through a rhythmic style known only to champions.

Poet U.B. was a featured author in *"Sincerely, Me"*, a book published by her brother and fellow author, Matthew Garcia. Her first solo self-published work entitled, *"The Left Side of Right"* explores domestic violence and the process of recovery. With her sophomore self-published work, *"Kolorblind Soul"*, U.B. shares a two-part poetry revolution.

U.B. intends to use her poetry to always pull the band aid off experiences that are often muted, ignored and very often fail to be recognized as problems in order to overcome hardships of the heart and soul and to teach others to be resilient.

For booking and information, contact: Poet U.B. via email Info@PoetUB.com

www.ingramcontent.com/pod-product-compliance
Lightning Source LLC
Chambersburg PA
CBHW050112170426
43198CB00014B/2542